# Sikhie Secrets:
# The Trinity

By
**Mike Bhangu**

**BBP**

Illustrator: Mike Singh Bhangu
Published by BB Productions
British Columbia, Canada
thinkingmanmike@gmail.com

Ik Onkar. Sat Naam.

# Table of Contents

Introduction
God's Name and The Word
More on God's Word
Society of Saints
Rebirth
How to Encounter Sat Guru
The Secret of Jivan Mukti
I Salute The Spirit
How Sat Guru Answers
Vibration Meditation
Amrit Vela
In and Outbound
Unknown Vibration
The Power of Kirtan
A Brief Description of God: Mool Mantra
What is Love?
Kali Yuga
Summation

## Introduction

This small collection of articles will primarily explore three of the foremost notions presented by the Sikh doctrine--Sat Guru, The Word, and The Name. They are considered the Sikh Trinity--the three points of the celestial triangle, and only through them, will a person attain Jivan Mukti. If an individual wishes to conquer mortality and the cycle of life and death, the Trinity must be understood.

The ideas set forth within this manuscript were inspired and expressed by *Sri Guru Granth Sahib Ji.* The citations are from an English version of *Sri Guru Granth Sahib Ji* and can be viewed at www.srigranth.org.

## God's Name and The Word

One idea of utmost importance, communicated by many, many Holy Books, but most explicitly by the Sikh Holy Text, *Sri Guru Granth Sahib,* is the value of God's Name and God's Word.

God's Name, or Sat Naam (True Name), is hidden within all creation. When revealed, it gifts the person with intuitive spiritual wisdom and mystical knowledge. Moreover, The Name is salvation, The Name is nirvana, and The Name is the cure for all ailments. The Name is so because it activates the unstruck sound current of "The Word" within a person.

The Name can be under as a specific sacred vibration, and as can The Word (The Shabad). When The Word is active within the body, it unlocks salvation, it unlocks nirvana, and it unlocks the all-in-one medicine.

> *"Whoever obtains the Naam, the Philosopher's Stone, becomes the embodiment of Truth, manifest and radiant throughout the world."*--(Sri Guru Granth Sahib Ji, ang 1392)

> *"Those who are attached to the Naam, the Name of the Lord, are saved; without the Name, they must go to the City of Death. O Nanak, without the Name, they find no peace; they come and go in reincarnation with regrets. ||24||"*--(Sri Guru Granth Sahib Ji, ang 1415)

The idea of The Word is within most religious doctrine and the vibration that is The Word, as with The Name, supports the constitution of everything that exists. Without this support, nothing, excluding God, can be.

The power of The Word is indescribable and from The Word comes all creation, within all creation is The Word, and in The Word all merge.

However, within a person, The Word is silent and must be triggered. When The Word is active in a person, it purifies the individual--he or she rises above the faults and duality of the mind and body, and he or she essentially merges with The Lord.

> *"In the beginning was the Word, and the Word was with God, and the Word was God."*--(John 1:1)

> *"...that by the word of God the heavens were of old, and the earth standing out of the water and in the water."*--(2 Peter 3:5)

> *"When the body dies, where does the soul go? It is absorbed into the untouched, unstruck melody of the Word of the Shabad."*--(Sri Guru Granth Sahib Ji, ang 327)

> *"The Unstruck Sound-current of the Shabad, the Word of God, vibrates in the Court of the Lord."*--(Sri Guru Granth Sahib Ji, ang 1137)

> *"Good deeds, righteousness and Dharmic faith, purification, austere self-discipline, chanting, intense meditation and pilgrimages to sacred shrines - all these abide in the Shabad."*--(Sri Guru Granth Sahib Ji, ang 1332)

> *"Attachment to Maya is burnt away by the Word of the Shabad."*--(Sri Guru Granth Sahib Ji, ang 1173)

> *"Those who die in the Word of the Shabad are saved. Without the Shabad, no one is liberated."*--( Sri Guru Granth Sahib Ji, ang 1416)

To activate The Word, The Name is required, and The Name is also within every person. However, as *Sri Guru Granth Sahib* emphasizes, God's Name is dormant until awoken and only God reveals God's Name. In specific, God Spiritually-Manifest. God is said to be

Unmanifest and Manifest, and "Sat Guru" (True Guru or Perfect Guru) is the term used by *Sri Guru Granth Sahib* to identify the second. This idea of God Unmanifest and Manifest is further explained in the upcoming article, "Rebirth".

> *"I am a sacrifice to my True Guru, who has revealed the Lord's hidden Name to me.||2||"*--(Sri Guru Granth Sahib Ji, ang 697)

> *"Without serving the True Guru, the Naam is not obtained. The Naam is the True profit in this world. || 6 || True is His Will, beauteous and pleasing through the Word of the Shabad. The Panch Shabad, the five primal sounds, vibrate and resonate."*--(Sri Guru Granth Sahib Ji, ang 1057)

*Sri Guru Granth Sahib* firmly believes that meditation on or contemplation of The Name and The Word have greater spiritual merit than any visit to a sacred place of pilgrimage, material object, prayer, posture, or Holy Book. The most exalted offering a person can make to The Eternal is The Name and The Word.

Meditation on or contemplation of The Name and The Word is important and not just solitary reflection. The practice, within a society of saints (Saadh Sangat or Sat Sangat), is highly valued by *Sri Guru Granth Sahib*. If you ever, by God's Grace, encounter a true society of saints, take the time to meditate with them. If you can, selflessly serve them. A true saint is immersed in The Name and The Word, and openly vibrates them. In such a state of being, their identical-self has consumed the self and there is little difference between him or her and The Great Architect. Tell me--is there any earthly person more worthy of selfless service?

> *"In the Saadh Sangat, the Company of the Holy, the Lord of the World is understood."*--(Sri Guru Granth Sahib Ji, ang 1156)

The notion that there is very little difference, if any, between God and those saints who have merged with The Lord isn't exclusive to the Sikh doctrine and I've encountered the idea in almost all the religions I've studied. Even in the New Testament the idea is found.

> *(Jesus said) "And he that seeth me seeth him that sent me." -*
> *-(John 12:45)*

> *(Jesus said) "I and my Father are one."--(John 10:30)*

> *(Jesus said) "Don't you believe that I am in the Father, and that the Father is in me? The words I say to you I do not speak on my own authority. Rather, it is the Father, living in me, who is doing his work."--(John 14:10)*

In this respect, Guru Nanak too was The Father. Guru Nanak too merged with The One.

The true saints are above the duality of the mind--they are egoless and absorbed in The Name and The Word. For them, the world exists, and by their angelic efforts, such as celestial meditation, the world continues to exist. If God has favourites, they are it, and among them, Sat Guru is. If you wish to find the Holy Spirit (Sat Guru), one method is to search out a society of saints. In the Saadh Sangat, Sat Guru plays.

> *"The Treasure of the Naam, the Name of the Lord, is found in the Saadh Sangat, the Company of the Holy."--*(Sri Guru Granth Sahib Ji, ang 1300)

> *"The Saadh Sangat, the Company of the Holy, is heaven itself. ||4||8||16||"--*(Sri Guru Granth Sahib Ji, ang 1161)

> *"The True Guru (Sat Guru) meditates on the Lord, the Primal Being. The Sat Sangat, the True Congregation, loves the True Guru. Those who join the Sat Sangat, and serve the*

*True Guru - the Guru unites them in the Lord's Union."*-- (Sri Guru Granth Sahib Ji, ang 1424)

The Name is salvation. The Name is nirvana. The Name is the cure for all ailments. The Name is so because it activates the unstruck sound current of "The Word" within the person.

*"O Nanak, through the Naam, glorious greatness is obtained; through the Word of the Guru's Shabad, the True One is found. ||4||3||"*--(Sri Guru Granth Sahib Ji, ang 1333)

## More on God's Word

For some reason, several religions promote the notion that the entirety of their principle Holy Book is The Word of God. However, the Holy Books do not associate The Word with the entirety of any Holy Book.

Moreover, the whole of a Holy Book consists of words and not just a single word. In the different books, within this context, when God's Word is described, it isn't pluralized, but religions associate God's Word with words, sentences, and paragraphs.

Yes, it's true and the phrase "God's words" is used in some of the Holy Books and that doesn't reference God's Word as a vibration. In addition, in the Old Testament and the New Testament, the notion of "God's Word" is applied in different ways and with different means. For that reason, there is confusion. At times, it refers to what God supposedly said to a person, and at other times it references God's Word as a primal sound or vibration--as the passages below illustrate. Moreover, it's clear that meaning was lost in translation and the English version of the New Testament doesn't give the same message as the New Testament in its original languages. My suspicion is that the originals are much clearer about this idea of God's Word as a vibration.

> *"The Word became flesh and made his dwelling among us."*--(John 1:14)

> *"...I have written unto you, young men, because ye are strong, and the word of God abideth in you, and ye have overcome the wicked one."*--(John 2:14)

> *"Wherefore lay apart all filthiness and superfluity of naughtiness, and receive with meekness the engrafted word, which is able to save your souls."*--(James 1:21)

> *"For the word of God is alive and active. Sharper than any double-edged sword, it penetrates even to dividing soul and*

*spirit, joints and marrow; it judges the thoughts and attitudes of the heart."*--(Hebrews 4:12)

*"The grass withers and the flowers fall, but the word of our God endures forever."*--(Isaiah 40:8)

*"Being born again, not of corruptible seed, but of incorruptible, by the word of God, which liveth and abideth for ever."*--(1 Peter 1:23)

Taken at face value, The Word, as expressed in all the different Holy Books, to one degree or another, positions a combination of sounds that form a word or a specific vibration.

The Word is an unknown vibration and religions promote an inaccurate description of it. The misconception alienates the person from the power of The Word and its potential to bestow salvation.

A theory of Quantum Mechanics, String Theory, suggests that extremely tiny string-like particles pervade and vibrate through everything within the Universe. The characteristics of these strings are very similar to the characteristics given to God's Word by the different Holy Books.

*"As long as the mortal does not come to understand the mystery of the Shabad, the Word of God, he shall continue to be tormented by death."*--(Sri Guru Granth Sahib Ji, ang 1126 of 1430)

## Society of Saints

*"The snake-charmer, by his spell, neutralizes the poison and leaves the snake without fangs. Just so, the Saints remove suffering; O Nanak, they are found by good karma.||16||"*-- (Sri Guru Granth Sahib Ji, ang 1361)

*"The four great blessings, and the eighteen supernatural spiritual powers - above all these are the Holy Saints."*--(Sri Guru Granth Sahib Ji, ang 1227)

*"I have heard that the most exalted Path of all is the Sangat, the Guru's Congregation. Joining it, the fear of death is taken away."*--(Sri Guru Granth Sahib Ji ,ang 1406)

*"Says Nanak, I am a sacrifice to the Saints, who are the Eternal Companions of God. ||2||3||"*--(Sri Guru Granth Sahib Ji, ang 1322)

*"Vibrating and meditating on the Lord of the Universe in the Saadh Sangat, O Nanak, the eternal place of rest is found.||4||"*--(Sri Guru Granth Sahib Ji, ang 1360)

*"O Lord, be merciful, and unite me with the Perfect Guru. Joining with the Sat Sangat, the True Congregation, I shall cross over the terrifying world-ocean. ||1||Pause||"*--(Sri Guru Granth Sahib Ji, ang 1134).

---

In the company of Saints, a person understands restraint, with little or no constraint. The angelic knowledge is quaint; the sacred paint behind the paint. Touch, see, and hear they can the faint.

Rebirth

After spending many years examining religions, I was blessed with a revelation, the awareness of God's Spirit.

A common understanding there is, God is Unmanifest and God is also Spiritually-Manifest. The Great Architect is in all creation and all creation is in The Great Architect--the Unmanifest aspect. Simultaneously, God is unto the self, outside all creation, and interacts with God Unmanifest--the Spiritually-Manifest aspect.

The idea of God Manifest is in almost all religions and in the *New Testament*, the *Old Testament*, and the *Qur'an*, the terms The Spirit, The Holy Spirit, and The Spirit of God signify the same as Sat Guru. Sat Guru (True Guru) is the name given by the Sikh Holy Book, *Sri Guru Granth Sahib Ji*, to denote the Manifest. The Buddhists know The Spirit as Maitreya. Thoth called The Manifest, Poimandres.

> *"Flesh gives birth to flesh, but the Spirit gives birth to spirit. You should not be surprised at my saying, 'You must be born again.' The wind blows wherever it pleases. You hear its sound, but you cannot tell where it comes from or where it is going. So it is with everyone born of the Spirit."*--(John 3:6-8)

> *"And Jesus, when he was baptized, went up straightway out of the water: and, lo, the heavens were opened unto him, and he saw the Spirit of God descending like a dove, and lighting upon him."*--(Matthew 3:16)

> *"When he and his servant arrived at Gibeah, a procession of prophets met him; the Spirit of God came powerfully upon him, and he joined in their prophesying."*--(Samuel 10:10)

> *"Therein descend angels and the Spirit by the command of their Lord--with every matter."*--(Qur'an 97:5)

Sometimes this notion of God Manifest isn't so easy to identify, and as author Alexander Smith suggests in his book, *The Holiest Lie Ever: Glorified by Myths, Mysticism, Symbolism, Rituals and Traditions,* the symbols of the dove and fire, at times, represent the Holy Spirit. These symbols can be found in a multitude of religions, including those of the ancient Greeks, the Romans, the Druids, the Egyptians, the Incas, the Hindus, the Buddhists, and the Celts, who claim their Salic Laws were guided by Sat Guru. The Celts named The Holy Spirit, Salo Ghost. Vishnu is the name given by the Hindu religion. Supposedly, this is a secret kept by the high caste Hindus--the Brahmins. But since I didn't learn from any clandestine school, I have no need to hide truths.

Although it might appear as if there are two, God Unmanifest and the Holy Spirit, there is actually only one. It's difficult to comprehend. A distinction there is and a distinction there isn't.

> *"The Guru is God, and God is the Guru, O Nanak; there is no difference between the two, O Siblings of Destiny. ||4||1||8||"*--(Sri Guru Granth Sahib Ji, ang 442 of 1430)

> *"There is no difference between the Supreme Lord God and the Guru. ||4||11||24||"*--(Sri Guru Granth Sahib Ji, ang 1142 of 1430)

That said, *Sri Guru Granth Sahib Ji* clearly draws a distinction between God Manifest and God Unmanifest.

> *"O Servant of the Lord, O True Guru, O True Primal Being, I offer my prayers to You, O Guru."*--(Sri Guru Granth Sahib Ji, ang 492 of 1430)

> *"Without the True Guru, no one has obtained the Lord; without the True Guru, no one has obtained the Lord."*--(Sri Guru Granth Sahib Ji, ang 466 of 1430)

*"O Nanak, by perfect good karma, you shall meet the True Guru, and then the Dear Lord, by His Sweet Will, shall bless you with His Mercy."*--(Sri Guru Granth Sahib Ji, ang 591 of 1430)

The person has the potential to build a relationship with God Manifest, but God Unmanifest cannot be found or understood solely by woman or man, and only Sat Guru can introduce a person to The Lord. Furthermore, God's Spirit is a teacher--the all-knowing and always truthful Professor. A lecture conducted by The Spirit will reveal reality's true nature. But only when the student is ready, will the teacher appear.

*"For God has revealed them to us by his Spirit. The Spirit searches all things, even the deep things of God."*--(1 Corinthians 2:10)

*"We have not received the spirit of the world but the Spirit who is from God, that we may understand what God has freely given us."*--(1 Corinthians 2:12)

To connect with Sat Guru, a person should meditate towards, treat all creation as one, sincerely beg The Lord, and do their best to be a God Conscious Citizen. Such a person is in a state of being ideal for a celestial experience. Their constitution produces a resonance Sat Guru favours. Without it, God Manifest doesn't approach.

*"For the sinful nature desires what is contrary to the Spirit, and the Spirit what is contrary to the sinful nature. They are in conflict with each other, so that you are not to do whatever you want."*--(Galatians 5:17)

The influence and instruction of Sat Guru is necessary to understand The Great Architect. Without it, no person will truly grasp the wonders of God. If a person were to forget all religion and entrust strictly in the Holy Spirit, they would gain enlightenment. The Holy Spirit taught all the prophets, even the wise Hermes Trismegistus was a student. He referred to God Manifest as Poimandres, the Great Dragon. For that reason, religions have much in common. The source was the same and the differences are earthly assertions.

The Perfect Guru teaches the person and no individual can truly understand the nature of reality without the Holy Spirit. But God's Spirit can do much more for the God seeker. Sat Guru can purify and unite.

In an instant, the Holy Spirit can transform the beliefs, thoughts, and wants of a person. That includes the neural pathways that facilitate them. The Spirit of God has the ability to bring a change to the body and mind, and that change is in harmony with the expectations of the Holy Spirit.

> *"But the fruit of the Spirit is love, joy, peace, patience, kindness, goodness, faithfulness."*--(Galatians 5:22)

The Spirit of God, first, cleanses by reprogramming the person to function through the better half of the mind and under the influence of the soul. The nature of the beautiful half gives life to the five weapons, which are: love, truth, contentment, compassion, and humility. The recoding also eliminates the mind's five thieves: lust, anger, attachment, ego, and greed. If a person's Karma permits, Sat Guru will go a step further and abolish the five weapons along with the five thieves. The five weapons too separate the person and Jivan Mukti (Salvation).

> *"He saved us, not because of righteous things we had done, but because of his mercy. He saved us through the washing of rebirth and renewal by the Holy Spirit."*--(Titus 3:5)

The Spirit of God has the power to set right the manner in which a person operates and a purification is a requirement before an individual can unite with The Formless. Consider this. The person is like a drop of water dyed with purple color, in a body of the clearest water. Until the purple color is removed from the droplet, it will never truly merge into the whole. Sat Guru eliminates that color. Without God's Spirit, regardless of how thin the color might get, the person will never truly merge.

God Unmanifest introduces God Spiritually-Manifest to the person, and the second unites the individual with God Unmanifest. That is, after a rebirth.

An individual may have mastered their chakras, learned how to manipulate the principles of the Universe so to perform miracles, or accumulated all the wealth the planet has to offer, but without Sat Guru, they will never merge with The Great Architect. Salo Ghost is the only able to blend a person with God, and that by activating God's Word and The Name. The Word and The Name are within every individual and their nature liberates the true self and provides a link to The Eternal.

---

*"The same was in the beginning with God. All things were made by him; and without him was not any thing made that was made. In him was life; and the life was the light of men. And the light shineth in darkness; and the darkness comprehended it not."*--(John 1:2-5)

## How to Encounter Sat Guru

All gifts worth holding rest with God Spiritually-Manifest and the Sikh philosophy aims to guide a person toward Sat Guru. This by revealing the wisdom required to experience an encounter with The Truest Teacher.

To experience a visit by Sat Guru, a person must correctly be, and suggestions such as the following create an invisible state of being Sat Guru favours. Every living thing emanates an invisible presence. However, until a person rises above the influences of the body and opens the Tenth Gate, the invisible will remain invisible.

1. Selfless service.
2. Egalitarianism.
3. Employment of the five weapons (love, truth, contentment, compassion, and humility).
4. Meditation.
5. Simran.
6. Kirtan.
7. Mantras (e.g. Mool Mantra).
8. Saintly companionship.

Sat Guru is attracted by the presence generated by the mentioned. An individual who adheres to the suggestions the Sikh doctrine forwards emanates a favourable vibration and, if Karma permits, the person will experience a visit by The True Guru. This is a natural law.

Just as the above suggestions produce the ideal state of being, a person can also create a presence that builds a barrier between Sat Guru and him or her. This too is a natural law and such examples as the following contaminate a person's state of being.

1. Alcohol, nicotine, and a meat-diet.
2. Corrupt company and degenerate establishments.
3. The five thieves (lust, anger, greed, ego, and attachment).

The Sikh dogma is designed to assist a person reach a state of being ideal for a celestial experience. To meet Sat Guru is one of the highest earthly purposes. The formula is simple but difficult to practice. Those who can are the best of the living.

Sat Guru can speak within a person and to a person. Sat Guru doesn't necessarily appear to an individual. Yet, do not confuse the inner dialogue the mind generates with instructions from Sat Guru. The voice of The True Teacher is distinct and sounds not where the mind's dialogue unfolds.

## The Secret of Jivan Mukti

A person's time and space of thought is influenced by two dominant databases of information. These two sources of information are the body and the spirit. The goal is to quiet the body's information so to allow the spirit's information to influence the time and space of thought. Only then is Jivan Mukti an exercisable option.

The body houses all sorts of information, some innate and some constructed. Constructed information is learned by an individual. Innate information is born with a person. The five thieves are innate and as are the five weapons. For this reason, the weapons must also be conquered. Yet, this doesn't mean a person transforms into a compassionless or loveless human. Far from, the compassion and love an individual experiences, after the body is quiet, is produced by the spirit and is pure. It is the truest form of love and compassion.

The goal is to quiet the body to allow the spirit to speak, and only The Word and The Name can permanently silence the body and release the spirit. However, no person will bask in these two sacred vibrations without Sat Guru. Only Sat Guru gifts The Word and The Name. The majority of the Sikh tenets are designed to guide a person to Sat Guru. It can be said that the sole purpose of the Sikh philosophy is to unite an individual with God's Spirit.

---

Love God and love all God's creations. In God's Mercy, the Lord will send The Spirit. Sat Guru truthfully teaches and Sat Guru can activate The Word within. The Word's resonance allows the "I" to experience the absolute reality. Through the mind of a mystic, union with The Great Architect can be achieved. A permanent love, in the truest sense, can soak through to every gene and every inch of a person's being. Salvation can be yours, and the first step is to believe.

## I Salute The Spirit

The person comes into the world innocent, with little knowledge of the reality cast into, and an individual learns of the world from the givers of information such as governments, movies, music, corporations, the family tree, and religions.

Regrettably, all of them have the potential to, purposely or accidentally, communicate inaccurate knowledge and a person can grow to live a life governed by an untruthful value system.

The consciousness can be misinformed and an individual can live a lie without knowing it. But there is a teacher forever truthful and who is eternally incorruptible. This giver of knowledge will never purposely or unknowingly mislead the individual. I forever salute Guru Nanak's Guru, the Holy Spirit.

---

*"Even if the mortal could reduce himself to the size of an atom, and through the ethers, worlds and realms, shoot in the blink of an eye, O Nanak, without the Holy Saint, he shall not be saved. ||2||"*--(Sri Guru Granth Sahib Ji, ang 1360)

## How Sat Guru Answers

Ask Sat Guru and you will receive an answer.

The distance between you and a direct answer depends on the cleanliness of your magnetic field. The cleaner and stronger a person's invisible presence, the more direct the answer.

A dirty and weak metaphysical presence welcomes indirect and obscure answers, and for an untrained mind, it will be difficult to identify this type of answer. The response might briefly flash before an individual, and in the form of a sentence, within a book. Or the answer might reveal itself through another person and the ideas he or she is sharing. Or the answer might be illustrated through the behaviour of birds. The list of indirect methods of delivering an answer is unending and God's Spirit can orchestrate any invisible and visible thing within the Universe to convey a reply.

Those individuals with a clean and strong invisible presence receive direct answers and the most direct answer manifests as an inner whisper. God's Spirit can speak to a person, and from within, a person will hear.

My friend, do your best to garnish and maintain a superior aura. If you can achieve this, anything you wish to know can be known, and it will be a matter of asking the right question.

## Vibration Meditation

There are many methods of meditation. The Sikh philosophy refers to several of them. One is a vibration meditation. This technique I learned from a Nihang Sikh.

This meditation method uses sounds, four sounds, and four areas of the body. Each sound should be produced or vibrated in one given area. The four sounds are "WA", "HE", "GU", "RU".

Vibrate "WA" in the area of the stomach, "HE" in the chest area, "GU" in the throat area, and "RU" as far up the head as possible.

Each area of vibration contains an energy center and vibrating the four sounds stimulates these centers.

While vibrating each sound, with your mind, focus on each area and the corresponding sound. Initially, practice vibrating each sound individually. Then, vibrate one after the other, in a smooth flow. During which, focus your mind toward The One.

The last vibration is the most difficult, and if it is correctly practiced, a nirvanic sensation will be felt near the forehead.

## Amrit Vela

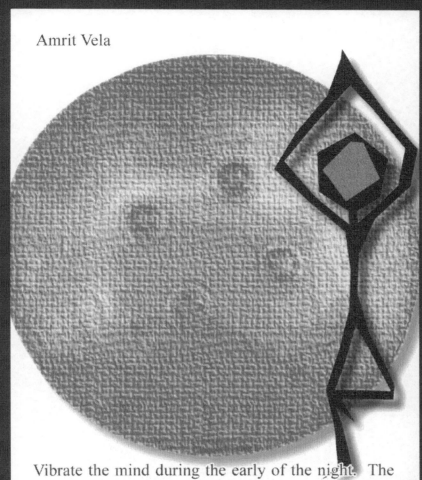

Vibrate the mind during the early of the night. The holy suggest that then is the ideal time to meditate. The reason being, the person isn't exposed to the rays of the Sun. The power of the Sun interferes with a meditative state. Moreover, the energy the Earth absorbed from the Sun, during the day, is released at night, but in a different form, and that energy is conducive to the practice of meditation.

## In and Outbound

A military mind and the soul of a saint,
with that, vibrate, meditate, vibrate, contemplate.
Release the self from traits like anger, lust, and hate.
Unearth the right frequency and, and meditate.
Negate the popular and let the mind vibrate.
Translate the light within and let the rest gradate.
Locate the right, the right frequency and equate;
with that, vibrate, meditate, vibrate, contemplate.

*In, in and outbound, meditate on strong ground.  Let the sound resound.
Within compound; rebound.  Be found by the renowned.  The greatest,
the greatest secret of Nanak's house.*

Use the five, the five weapons of peace.
With time, experience a caprice;
a release from the mind's inner grease.
The experienced can't disagree.
The weapons allow the "I" to see.
The other five blur reality--
trapping the "I" to secular things.

*In, in and outbound, meditate on strong ground.  Let the sound resound.
Within compound; rebound.  Be found by the renowned.  The greatest,
the greatest secret of Nanak's house.*

*"Prays Nanak, the True Guru has taught me this, to vibrate
and meditate forever on the Lord of the Universe.
||4||1||3||"*--(Sri Guru Granth Sahib Ji, ang 779)

Unknown Vibration

The Ida and the Pingali are instruments--pathways within the human. Inhale through them to awaken the celestial serpent. The "True Guru" will compliment.

The "True Guru" is God Manifest. There are two halves to the one beginning and end. Deathless and my mind can't comprehend. Everything is a vibration.

Near the white light of the saintly, the undertaking is easy. A proven methodology; the invisible turns worthy. Even the grimy are set free, in the presence of the holy.

*"Says Nanak, True is the Kirtan of the Lord's Praise."*--(Sri Guru Granth Sahib Ji, ang 1157 of 1430)

## The Power of Kirtan

Selfless service; restraint of the senses; and contemplation/meditation on the True Name, The Shabad, Sat Guru, and The Eternal are the highest forms of worship, and comparable is Kirtan. Kirtan is the singing of the Lord's praises.

*"The Lord's servant sings the Kirtan of His Praises as his worship, deep meditation, self-discipline and religious observances."*--(Sri Guru Granth Sahib Ji, ang 498)

*"Your humble servant, who obtains the Medicine of the Naam, is rid of the illnesses of countless lifetimes and incarnations. So sing the Kirtan of the Lord's Praises, day and night. This is the most fruitful occupation."*--(Sri Guru Granth Sahib Ji, ang 107-108)

*"In this Dark Age of Kali Yuga, the Kirtan of the Lord's Praise has appeared as a Light in the world. How rare are those few Gurmukhs who swim across to the other side! The Lord bestows His Glance of Grace; O Nanak, the Gurmukh receives the jewel."*--(Sri Guru Granth Sahib Ji, ang 145)

As spoken of by *Guru Granth Sahib Ji*, the benefits of Kirtan are:

*"When the Saints became kind and compassionate, they told me this. Understand, that whoever sings the Kirtan of God's Praises, has performed all religious rituals. || 2 ||"*--(Sri Guru Granth Sahib Ji, ang 902)

*"Sing the Kirtan, the Praises of the Lord, the Giver of peace, the Destroyer of pain; He shall bless you with perfect spiritual wisdom. Sexual desire, anger and greed shall be*

43

*shattered and destroyed, and your foolish ego will be dispelled."*--(Sri Guru Granth Sahib Ji, ang 979)

*"Without the Lord's Name, flavors are tasteless and insipid. Sing the Sweet Ambrosial Praises of the Lord's Kirtan; day and night, the Sound-current of the Naad will resonate and resound."*--(Sri Guru Granth Sahib Ji, ang 1219)

The term "Naad" refers to the unheard celestial sound produced by the Shabad. The Word is a composition of the five primal sounds.

*"The Panch Shabad, the five primal sounds, echo the perfect sound current of the Naad. The wondrous, amazing unstruck melody vibrates."*--(Sri Guru Granth Sahib Ji, ang 888)

*"The True Guru is the All-knowing Primal Being; He shows us our true home within the home of the self. The Panch Shabad, the Five Primal Sounds, resonate and resound within; the insignia of the Shabad is revealed there, vibrating gloriously."*--(Sri Guru Granth Sahib Ji, ang 1291)

*Sri Guru Granth Sahib Ji* tells that when Naad is heard, pure peace and bliss are experienced. Naad can be heard by repeating The Name of God.

*"Repeating the Naam, the Unstruck Sound-current of the Naad resounds."*--(Sri Guru Granth Sahib Ji, ang 1144)

*"The Naam is my food and love. The Naam is the objective of my mind. By the Grace of the Saints, I never forget the Naam. Repeating the Naam, the Unstruck Sound-current of the Naad resounds."*--(Sri Guru Granth Sahib Ji, ang 1144)

Kirtan has many benefits, and along with the mentioned, the sounds and vibrations created by the type of kirtan prescribed by *Guru Granth Sahib Ji,* strengthens a person's magnetic field.

Every person, thing, and place emanates a magnetic field, or what some might call an aura, and a person's magnetic field influences his or her thoughts, actions, health, luck, and the type of experiences an individual will attract. The stronger a person's aura, the higher degree of positivity he or she will encounter, and the stronger the magnetic field, the less negative entities are able to influence the subtle nature of an individual.

The human being has two natures, the physical and the subtle, and the latter can be influenced by sounds and vibrations. Since the physical and the subtle are interrelated, a change in the invisible component of the person naturally influences the physical half of the human. Using a candle flame, Swami Murugesu's *Flame Experiment* demonstrated the impact of certain sounds on the subtle and the material. Given specific sounds, the color of the flame would change, and as would its overall presence.

Everything in existence was first a metaphysical thing, spirit, then the physical dimension evolved from it, and all material things exist within the parameters of their subtle essence. The mystics of the world, past and present, are able to perceive the invisible nature of existence, and they can also influence this essence. If a mystic wishes to influence a material thing, he or she first manipulates the subtle essence. The invisible component to everything that exists rests in what some call the Astral Plane. This plane of existence occupies the same space as the material. If a mystic desires to, for example, heal a sick person, he or she will enter the Astral Plane and repair the subtle nature of the person, so to heal their physical component.

Selfless service; restraint of the senses; and contemplation/meditation on the True Name, The Shabad, Sat Guru, and The Eternal are the highest forms of worship, and comparable is Kirtan.

The teachings within *Sri Guru Granth Sahib Ji* are the teachings of Sat Guru, and the Gurudawara is the doorway to the True Guru. There, The Lord's praises are meant to be sung.

> *"At the Gurdwara, the Guru's Gate, the Kirtan of the Lord's Praises are sung. Meeting with the True Guru, one chants the Lord's Praises. The True Guru eradicates sorrow and suffering, and bestows honor in the Court of the Lord. || 4 || The Guru has revealed the inaccessible and unfathomable Lord. The True Guru returns to the Path, those who have wandered away. No obstacles stand in the way of devotion to the Lord, for one who serves the Guru. The Guru implants perfect spiritual wisdom."--(Sri Guru Granth Sahib Ji, ang 1075)*

## A Brief Description of God: Mool Mantra

*"By thinking, He cannot be reduced to thought, even by thinking hundreds of thousands of times."*--(Sri Guru Granth Sahib Ji, ang 1 of 1430)

The following prayer/mantra was written by Guru Nanak and inspired by Sat Guru. This mantra is a brief description of God, and simultaneously, it reveals the nature of the cosmos.

Ik Onkar. Sat Naam. Kartaa Purakh. Nirbhau. Nirvair. Akaal Moorat. Ajooni Saibhang. Gurprasad.

*"Ik: There is ONE (Ik) reality, the origin and the source of everything. The creation did not come out of nothing. When there was nothing, there was ONE, Ik.*

*Onkar: When Ik becomes the creative principal it becomes Onkar. Onkar manifests as visible and invisible phenomenon. The creative principle is not separated from the created--it is present throughout the creation in an unbroken form, 'kaar'.*

*Sat Naam: The sustaining principle of Ik is Sat Naam, the True Name.*

*Kartaa Purakh: Ik Onkar is Creator (Purakh) and Doer (Kartaa) of everything.*

*Nirbhau: That Ik Onkar is devoid of any fear, because there is nothing but itself.*

*Nirvair: That Ik Onkar is devoid of any enmity, because there is nothing but itself.*

*Akaal Moorat: That Ik Onkar is beyond Time (Akaal) and yet existing.*

*Ajooni: That Ik Onkar does not condense and come into any birth. All the phenomenon of birth and death of forms are within it.*

*Saibhang: That Ik Onkar exists on its own, by its own. It is not caused by anything before it or beyond it.*

*Gurprasaad: That Ik Onkar expresses itself through God-Manifest, known as Sat Guru. Through the Lord's grace and mercy (Prasaad) this happens."*

(Source: http://www.sikhiwiki.org/index.php/Mool_Mantar)

The above Mool Mantra is the popular version, and several people believe, including myself, that the following was initially the ending of this mantra. I support this position simply because without the following additions, the mantra feels incomplete and abruptly ends.

Jap. Aad sach. Jugaad sach. Hai bhee sach. Nanak hose bhee sach.

*Jap: Chant*
*Aad sach: True in the Primal Beginning.*
*Jugaad sach: True throughout the different epochs.*
*Hai bhee sach: True here and now.*
*Nanak hosee bhee sach: Forever true, says Nanak.*

This mantra is extremely powerful and all mantras, prayers, or music written by a truly holy person, through whom God speaks, are so because the holy individual combined specific sounds together to make celestial sentences and these sounds power-up a person's magnetic field. A strong magnetic field is the key to a good life.

## What is Love?

The craving that each living thing has, the yearning for something—a union—a completion, commonly misidentified by the contemporary person with a love for a material object or another human, is an innate desire to reunite with The Unmanifest. This is why a material object or a person can't permanently satisfy the craving. A material object or a person only disguises the feeling, like a pharmaceutical painkiller. When the mind has grown accustom to the material object or person, the yearning will again speak to the time and space of thought. Only The Source can provide an unbreakable and everlasting love. Only The Great Architect can satisfy the inner impulse.

# LOVE
# BE LOVED
# LIVE

Love God and be a God Conscious Citizen. In God's Mercy, the Lord will send the Spirit. God's Spirit truthfully teaches, and the Spirit can give The Name of God while activating The Word within. The Word's resonance allows the "I" to experience the absolute reality. That experience can bestow salvation (union with The Great Architect) on any living thing. A permanent love, in the truest sense, can be achieved.

## Kali Yuga

According to Eastern religious philosophy, the world continuously cycles through four ages, and each era produces a different type of civilization, as determined by the distance between humanity and God. In the first age, the people are closest to God and there exists only one religion. All people have God knowledge and all people are wardens of a God-Consciousness. But with each proceeding age, the people regress and move further from God, God knowledge, and a God-Consciousness. According to Sikh teachings, humanity is currently in the fourth era, the Age of Kali Yuga.

The forth epoch is said to be the darkest of all and furthest from the era of perfect existence. It is a time of dark influences and home to untruths. To one degree or another, almost all institutions facilitate falsehoods. That includes the culture and the intelligence filled and shaped by those institutions, and every person who makes contact with them. Furthermore, the universe is predisposed to sway a person's consciousness to favour the five thieves over the five weapons.

The four ages are: The Golden Age of Sat Yuga, the Silver Age of Trayta Yuga (Ram existed in this era), the Brass Age of Dwaapar Yuga (Krishna existed in this era), and the Iron Age of Kali Yuga (also called the Age of Darkness).

> *"In the Golden Age of Sat Yuga, everyone embodied contentment and meditation; religion stood upon four feet. With mind and body, they sang of the Lord, and attained supreme peace. In their hearts was the spiritual wisdom of the Lord's Glorious Virtues. Their wealth was the spiritual wisdom of the Lord's Glorious Virtues; the Lord was their success, and to live as Gurmukh was their glory. Inwardly and outwardly, they saw only the One Lord God; for them there was no other second. They centered their consciousness lovingly on the Lord, Har, Har. The Lord's Name was their companion, and in the Court of the Lord,*

*they obtained honor. In the Golden Age of Sat Yuga, everyone embodied contentment and meditation; religion stood upon four feet. || 1 || Then came the Silver Age of Trayta Yuga; men's minds were ruled by power, and they practiced celibacy and self-discipline. The fourth foot of religion dropped off, and three remained. Their hearts and minds were inflamed with anger. Their hearts and minds were filled with the horribly poisonous essence of anger. The kings fought their wars and obtained only pain. Their minds were afflicted with the illness of egotism, and their self-conceit and arrogance increased. If my Lord, Har, Har, shows His Mercy, my Lord and Master eradicates the poison by the Guru's Teachings and the Lord's Name. Then came the Silver Age of Trayta Yuga; men's minds were ruled by power, and they practiced celibacy and self-discipline. || 2 || The Brass Age of Dwaapar Yuga came, and people wandered in doubt. The Lord created the Gopis and Krishna. The penitents practiced penance, they offered sacred feasts and charity, and performed many rituals and religious rites. They performed many rituals and religious rites; two legs of religion dropped away, and only two legs remained. So many heroes waged great wars; in their egos they were ruined, and they ruined others as well. The Lord, Compassionate to the poor, led them to meet the Holy Guru. Meeting the True Guru, their filth is washed away. The Brass Age of Dwaapar Yuga came, and the people wandered in doubt. The Lord created the Gopis and Krishna. || 3 || The Lord ushered in the Dark Age, the Iron Age of Kali Yuga; three legs of religion were lost, and only the fourth leg remained intact. Acting in accordance with the Word of the Guru's Shabad, the medicine of the Lord's Name is obtained. Singing the Kirtan of the Lord's Praises, divine peace is obtained. The season of singing the Lord's Praise has arrived; the Lord's Name is glorified, and the Name of the Lord, Har, Har, grows in the field of the body. In the Dark Age of Kali Yuga, if one plants any other seed than the*

*Name, all profit and capital is lost. Servant Nanak has found the Perfect Guru, who has revealed to him the Naam within his heart and mind. The Lord ushered in the Dark Age, the Iron Age of Kali Yuga; three legs of religion were lost, and only the fourth leg remained intact.  || 4 || 4 || 11 ||"*--(Sri Guru Granth Sahib Ji, ang 445-446 of 1430)

The term "Guru", used in the above passage, refers to God's Spirit and not a person.  The name "Har, Har" is a name used to describe God.  The Sikh Holy Text uses many different names to reference God.

This idea of the four ages is not exclusive to Sikhie thought and it's a very ancient idea that predates the oldest literature in the world, the Vedic literature.

There are a few theories to how long each epoch will last.  Some suggest 100 000s of years.  In specific, certain schools believe that the Golden Age lasts for 1 728 000 years, the Silver for 1 296 000 years, the Bronze for 864 000 years, and the Dark lasts 432 000 years.  Others suggest a Comic Year—about 26 000 Earth years.

There are two suppositions to what happens after this age.  One suggests that the cycle starts again with Sat Yuga.  Another theory suggests that the cycle doesn't begin again with Sat Yuga but instead descends after Kali Yuga passes.

The ancient Egyptians, Greeks, Mayans, and Romans too valued this idea of the different epochs, with Greek philosophy hosting an additional age, the Age of Heroes.  They even possessed maps of a world before the transition to the current age.  On those maps, Antarctica isn't covered by ice and the above sea land mass is much larger.  The Piri Reis Map and the Oronteus Finaeus Map, among others, are said to originate from those ancient maps.

Interestingly, the theory of the four ages provides an answer to a question mainstream historians are troubled by.  They don't know or don't believe how the early civilizations, such as the Egyptians, gained the knowledge that allowed them to spontaneously civilize. They've even gone as far as to suggest that aliens were responsible for their advancement. But according to the ancient Egyptians, the knowledge required to civilize came from the previous ages, and it was knowledge that survived the transition from one era to another. The Sphinx is said to be from the previous age. Geologists have determined that the Sphinx is actually older than 10 000 years. They've determined that by examining the weathering the Sphinx has experienced. The examination determined that at one point, the Sphinx was exposed to rain, and the Sahara hasn't experienced a rainfall in over 10 000 years. If this is true, then the civilizations of this age are not as advanced as the civilizations of the past. We're playing catch-up. The supposition reminds me of a particular idea found in the Christian doctrine:

*"What has been is what will be, and what has been done is what will be done; there is nothing new under the sun."*-- (Ecclesiastes 1:4-11)

It should be mentioned that before the introduction of each of the four eras, and before an age begins a decline, there happens a large-scale catastrophic event such as a deluge that erases the majority of a civilization (people, culture, architecture, knowledge, technology, etc). Catastrophic world events take place before the introduction of an era to wipe clear what is. Each era gives birth to a new type of civilization, and for the new to fully be, in this case, the old must first be near-erased. The Mayans believed that human civilizations have been wiped-out five times already. Ancient cultures from around the world also claim that civilizations were annihilated. For example, the Sumer story of Ziusudra, the Indian story of Manu, the Greek story of Deucalion, the Babylonian story of Utnapishtim, and the Hebrew story of Noah all describe civilization-destroying catastrophes.

In each age, the alignment of the planets is different from the others, and it's the change in the arrangement of the planets that stimulates catastrophic world events. In the Age of Sat Yug, in relation to the earth, Venus and Saturn play a much more dominant role. The symbol of Islam reflects that idea. Supposedly, the symbol is not of the Moon and Sun, but of Venus and Saturn.

Other mysteries are also put into perspective when the theory of the four ages is applied to them. For example, the questions surrounding some of the megalithic structures found all over the world become less when considering the eras. It's possible that they were designed the sizes they were, in a previous age, to survive catastrophic world events brought forth by the transition from one epoch to another. Perhaps, the heavens inspired as they motivated Noah, but instead of a boat, instructions were provided to build huge stone structures.

Whereas ships such as Noah's stored life, the megalithic structures of the world might be designed to give knowledge. They just have to be looked at in the right light. For example, they give accurate astrological readings, their proportions are precise and mathematically arranged, they exhibit signs that advanced technology was used to make them, and they're built on what the Chinese call dragon lines (earth energy lines). It's also possible they were designed to store written knowledge in the form of books and such, and that knowledge was retrieved after a catastrophic event. Perhaps, a storehouse of knowledge is yet to be recovered.

Ships and megalithic buildings are not the only type of structures supposedly inspired by the heavens to survive an upcoming natural disaster. For example, in the second chapter of the *Vendidad*, a division of the Zoroastrian holy book *Avesta,* God warned the Persian King Yima, the son of Vivanghat, of an upcoming natural disaster. God further instructed him to build underground cities and take shelter. Derinkuyu, the massive underground city discovered in Turkey, which can house as many as twenty thousand people and the required livestock, is said to be one of the cities Yima built.

Elaborate underground cities, complexes, and tunnel systems are not all that strange. The ancient cultures from all over the world have one story or another detailing such things. For example, the Hopi and the Apache Indians believe that their ancestors once lived underground, and only after a great calamity, did they resurface.

In his book, *Weird America*, Jim Brandon shares the legend of the city underneath California's Death Valley called "Shin-Au-Av". The story originates from the Paiute Indians, and supposedly, in this mysterious underground complex, once lived an unknown race of people. The Sioux Indians also share an underground city story, in which one of their people, White Horse, accidentally found an underground city occupied by strange humans. These underground humans gave White Horse a mystical talisman capable of melting rocks.

There are numerous stories from all over the world detailing the existence of underground cities, complexes, and tunnels. The two most famous hidden underground cities are Agharta and Shambhala.

According to Eastern religious philosophy, the world continuously cycles through four ages and humanity is currently in the fourth, the Age of Iron. In this era, Guru Nanak came, and in this age, only The Name and The Word can save.

The New Testament too expresses the idea of Ages, but the notion was lost in translation, and the following passage is plausibly inaccurate.

> *"Teaching them to observe all things whatsoever I have commanded you: and, lo, I am with you always, even unto the end of the world. Amen."*--(Matthew 28:20)

The word "world", in the above passage, is mistranslated and if correctly translated the word would be "aeon". So, the passage should read:

> *"Teaching them to observe all things whatsoever I have commanded you: and, lo, I am with you always, even unto the end of the aeon. Amen."*--(Matthew 28:20)

The mistranslations in the New Testament limit the Christian understanding of the Universe, and because of the above mistranslation, the Christian world, who read the English version of the New Testament, see the end of this Epoch as the end of human existence--the infamous End Days. However, the end of this Age is not the end of humanity and it is only the end of this type of human living and being.

## Summation

If the goal is Jivan Mukti, then one must walk in the direction of the Trinity--Sat Guru, Shabad, Sat Naam. Most other doctrinal prescriptions are there to guide a person to the Trinity. Such things as operating through the five weapons, selfless service, kirtan, meditation, saintly companionship, and mantras help create the ideal vibration. This resonance is favoured by Sat Guru and only Sat Guru reveals the Shabad and Sat Naam. Only through the Shabad and Sat Naam, is there hope for salvation.

30687101R00038

Made in the USA
San Bernardino, CA
28 March 2019